Nelson

English

Developing
Non-fiction Skills

BOOK ONE

John Jackman   Wendy Wren

Nelson

Contents

Unit	DEVELOPMENT Text	SKILLS Word	
1 Homes	Homes Around the World	Alphabetical order	'o-e' and 'oa' letter patterns
2 Fairy Stories	The Grimm Brothers	Alphabetical order	'ai' and 'air' letter patterns
3 Animal Homes	Rabbits	Alphabetical order	'le' letter pattern
4 Weather	A Contents Page	A thesaurus	'ea' letter pattern
5 Animals	A Day at the Zoo	Using a dictionary	Suffixes
6 Magic	The Vanishing Key Trick	Using a dictionary	Contractions
7 Mazes	The Maze Game	Definitions	Singular and plural nouns
8 Hands	Dirty Hands	Antonyms	Compound words
9 Parties	A Birthday Party	Common expressions	Words within words
10 Storms	Hurricane!	Adjectives	Prefixes
11 Books	Finding a Book	Using a dictionary	'ary', 'ery', 'ory' word endings
12 Tea	All About Tea	Using an index	Letter blends
Check-up			

Homes Around the World

These pictures show you different types of home from around the world.

Hong Kong is quite a small place and there is not much land to build on. Some people in Hong Kong live on boats like these, called junks.

These houses are in Bangkok, the capital of Thailand. They are on stilts because they are built over water.

Many Bedouin people live in the desert in Saudi Arabia. Traditionally, they have lived in tents because they move from place to place looking for water.

In hot countries like Africa, people often use mud to build houses because there is plenty of it, it costs nothing and it bakes hard in the sun.

Comprehension

A Look carefully at the pictures and captions on page 4.
Write a sentence to answer each question.

1 Where would you find junks?
2 Why do people live in junks?
3 What is unusual about some of the houses in Bangkok?
4 What sort of houses do some Bedouin people have?
5 Why do people in Africa often make their houses from mud?

Here is a description of a house from a book called *A Long Journey*.

Sulim climbed out of the car and looked at the house that was to be her new home. It was very different from the house where she had lived in India. That house had been long and low with thick, white walls and a big porch which shaded the house from the hot sun.

This house was made of red bricks. It was very tall and narrow with a chimney pot at one end of the roof. The door was painted bright red and had a big brass knocker. Nobody had lived in the house for a very long time and it had a sad look about it. Sulim was not sure if she was going to like living there.

Comprehension

B Read the extract from *A Long Journey*.
Write a sentence to answer each question.

1 Where had Sulim come from?
2 What did her first home look like?
3 What did her new home look like?
4 How did Sulim feel about her new home?

C Write sentences to answer these questions.

1 Is the passage on page 4 fact or fiction? How can you tell?
2 Is the extract from *A Long Journey* fact or fiction? How can you tell?

Vocabulary

Alphabetical order

Here are the 26 letters of the **alphabet**:

a b c d e f g h i j k l m n o p q r s t u v w x y z

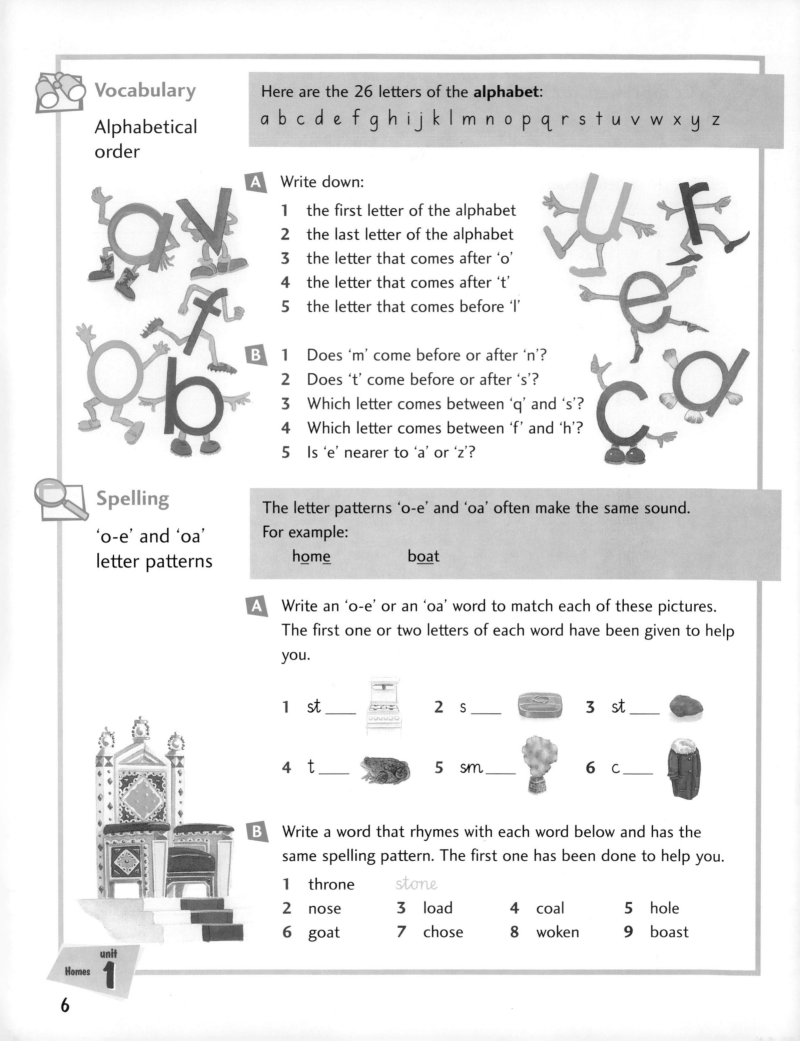

A Write down:

1 the first letter of the alphabet
2 the last letter of the alphabet
3 the letter that comes after 'o'
4 the letter that comes after 't'
5 the letter that comes before 'l'

B
1 Does 'm' come before or after 'n'?
2 Does 't' come before or after 's'?
3 Which letter comes between 'q' and 's'?
4 Which letter comes between 'f' and 'h'?
5 Is 'e' nearer to 'a' or 'z'?

Spelling

'o-e' and 'oa' letter patterns

The letter patterns 'o-e' and 'oa' often make the same sound.
For example:

h<u>o</u>m<u>e</u>   b<u>oa</u>t

A Write an 'o-e' or an 'oa' word to match each of these pictures.
The first one or two letters of each word have been given to help you.

1 st ____   2 s ____   3 st ____

4 t ____   5 sm ____   6 c ____

B Write a word that rhymes with each word below and has the
same spelling pattern. The first one has been done to help you.

1 throne   *stone*
2 nose   **3** load   **4** coal   **5** hole
6 goat   **7** chose   **8** woken   **9** boast

Grammar

Nouns

Nouns are naming words.

A **noun** is the name of a person, place or thing.
For example:

house   tent   car

A Write down the words from the box that are nouns.

town	door	water	move	flying
under	mud	make	man	hot
find	woman	flower	build	sun

B Look at the picture at the bottom of this page.
Copy the sentences below and choose a noun from the box
to fill each gap.

crane	girders	lorry	digger
men	wall	bricks	hole

1 The _____ is making a big _____ in the ground.

2 A _____ is delivering _____.

3 Heavy _____ are being lifted by a _____.

4 Three _____ are painting a _____.

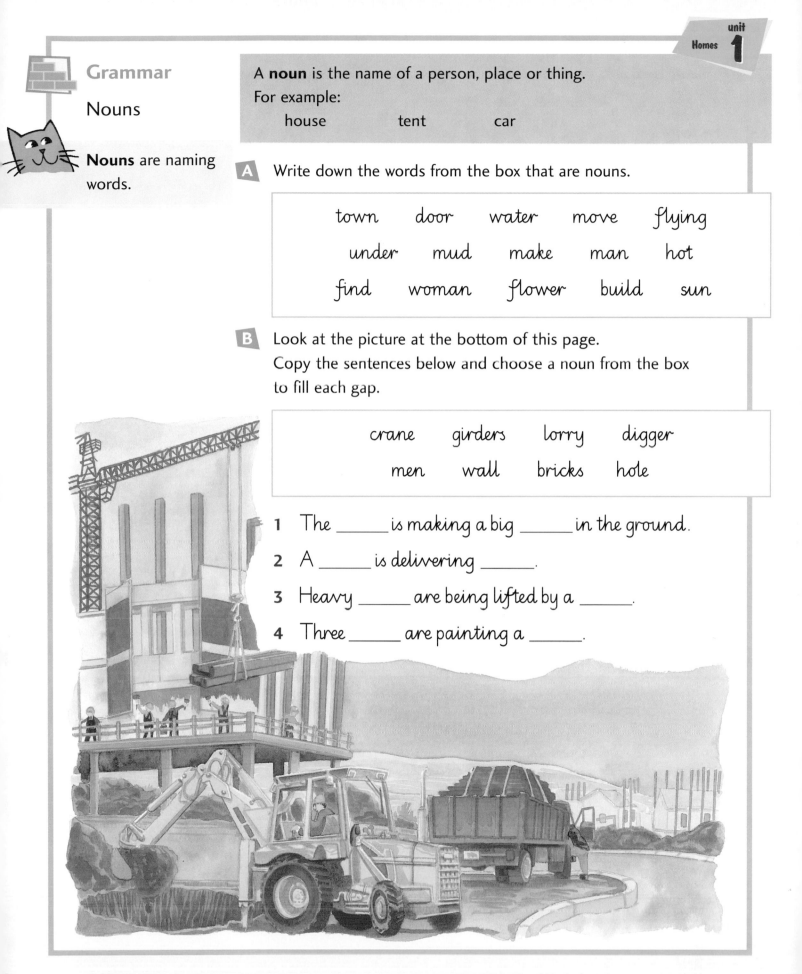

Punctuation

What is a sentence?

A **sentence** should begin with a **capital letter** and end with a **full stop**.
For example:

<u>T</u>hese boats are called junks<u>.</u>

capital letter　　　　　　full stop

A Copy the sentences below, putting in the capital letters and full stops.

1 she climbed out of the car

2 this house was made of red bricks

3 it had a chimney pot on the roof

4 nobody had lived there for a long time

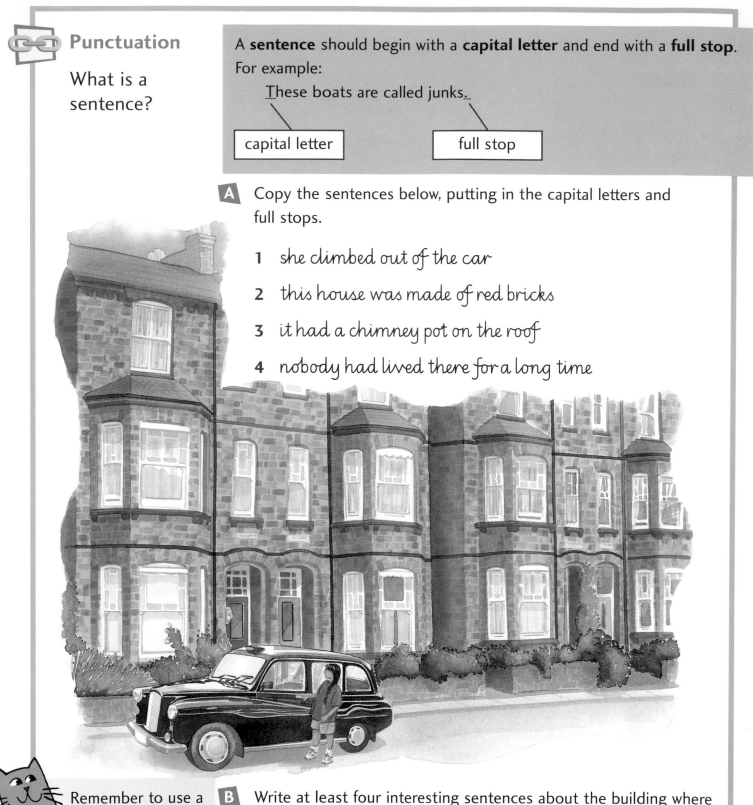

Remember to use a capital letter and a full stop for each sentence.

B Write at least four interesting sentences about the building where you live.

Writing

Fact and fiction

Books that are **factual** give us information. They are true.
Fiction books tell us imaginary things. They have been made up.

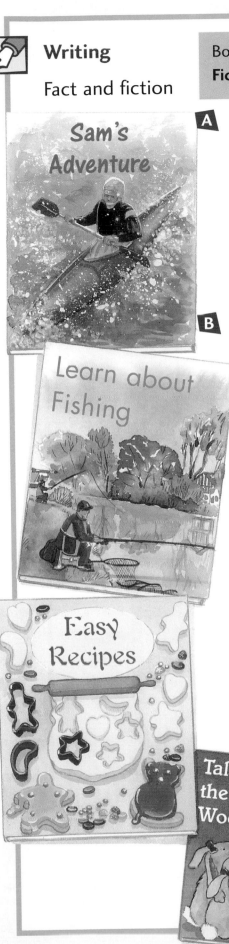

A Look at these book titles.

1 Copy the title of each book and, next to it, write whether you think it is fact or fiction.

2 a Write the heading 'Factual writing'. Make a list of as many different types of factual book as you can think of.

   b Make a list of as many types of book as you can think of that contain fiction.

B 1 Write some 'facts' about your family or the people you live with. You could:

- write how many brothers and sisters you have;
- write what their names are;
- describe your Mum, Dad or another adult you live with;
- write about your grandparents or your uncles and aunts.

2 You are going to write the beginning of a story about a boy called Danny. The story starts like this:

'My name is Danny. I have three brothers and two sisters…'

Write some more of the story. You need to write as though you are Danny, describing your brothers and sisters.

Remember, a story is fiction, so you can:

- use any names you want for the brothers and sisters;
- make them any age you want;
- describe them in any way you want.

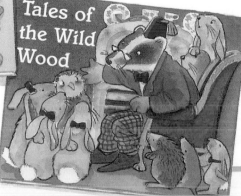

The Grimm Brothers

Many fairy tales are familiar to us thanks to two German brothers, called Jacob and Wilhelm Grimm. Jacob was born in 1785 and died in 1863. Wilhelm was born in 1786 and died in 1859.

Although we say that the Grimm brothers wrote these fairy tales, what they did was to talk to many older German people. They asked them about the old stories their parents had told them when they were children. The brothers listened to the stories, wrote them down and published them in a book called *Grimm's Fairy Tales* in 1812.

One of the best-known stories today is 'Hansel and Gretel'. It tells the story of two children whose parents can't afford to feed them, and leave the children in a forest. There, Hansel and Gretel meet a witch and only just escape being cooked in her oven!

Some of the other famous stories that the Grimms collected are 'Little Red Riding Hood', 'Tom Thumb' and 'The Frog Prince'.

Jacob and Wilhelm Grimm

Comprehension

A Copy and complete the sentences below.

1 Jacob and Wilhelm Grimm wrote many _____ _____.

2 Jacob and Wilhelm talked to many German _____, who told them _____ _____.

3 The Grimms wrote a book called _____ _____ _____.

4 'Hansel and Gretel' is a story about two _____.

5 The children only just _____ being cooked in a witch's oven.

B 1 Who was the older of the Grimm brothers?
2 How old was Jacob when he died?
3 How old was Wilhelm when he died?
4 Write what you think is the meaning of each term below.
   a fairy tales   b published   c collected

C There are four paragraphs in the passage 'The Grimm Brothers'. On a table like the one below, write what each paragraph is about. Use as few words as possible. The first one has been done to help you.

Paragraph	What it is about
1	Jacob and Wilhelm wrote fairy stories. Dates when they were born and died.

Vocabulary

Alphabetical order

A **dictionary** is a book that tells you the spellings and meanings of words.

The words in a dictionary are in **alphabetical order**. Words starting with 'a' come first, words starting with 'b' come second, words starting with 'c' come third, and so on. Words starting with 'z' come last. For example:

bed   chair   door

a b c d e f g h i j k l m n o p q r s t u v w x y z

A Write each group of letters in alphabetical order.

1 t l f r

2 s h l y w

3 G Q P L B A

4 U T X N A J

5 the letters of your first name

B Write each group of words in the order that you would find them in a dictionary.

1 fairy   story   brother

2 leaf   tree   branch

3 supper   bread   loaf

Spelling

'ai' and 'air' letter patterns

The letter pattern 'ai' usually makes a sound like the name of the first letter of the alphabet. For example:

p<u>ai</u>l   p<u>ai</u>d   p<u>ai</u>n

A Write down the words from the box that have the 'a' sound, like 'pail' and 'pain'.

snail   hair   stairs   aim   air   maid   fairy   rail   sailor   aid

B **1** Write down the words from the box above that **don't** have the 'a' sound.

2 What do you notice about the words you wrote down for question 1?

3 Write a sentence that includes at least three words with the 'air' letter pattern.

Grammar

Proper nouns

Remember, a **noun** is the name of a person, place or thing.

For example:

    fairy   brother   shoe

A **proper noun** is a special naming word. Proper nouns include people's names, place names and the names of special days. Proper nouns start with a capital letter. For example:

    <u>Jacob</u> lived in <u>Germany</u>.

'Jacob' is a proper noun.

It is someone's name.

'Germany' is a proper noun.

It is the name of a country.

A Copy these sentences. Underline the proper nouns.

1 Jacob and Wilhelm were brothers.

2 They lived in Germany.

3 They wrote a story about a boy called Tom Thumb.

4 The Grimm brothers also wrote about two children, Hansel and Gretel.

B 1 Look at the words in the box. Write down the proper nouns.

Remember to give each **proper noun** a capital letter.

> cinderella   grimm   story   wilhelm
>
> publish   scotland   fairy   spain   manchester
>
> book   giant   jacob

2 Copy and complete these sentences.

a My name is _____ .

b My teacher's name is _____ .

c I like shopping at _____ .

d The street where I live is called _____ .

Punctuation

Speech

Remember, when people speak, we sometimes show what they say in speech bubbles. For example:

What is your favourite story, Jeev?

I like 'Tom Thumb' best, but I like lots of others as well.

Jake

Jeev

A 1 Write the words in the speech bubble that Jake spoke.
2 What did Jeev reply?

Don't forget the capital letters and full stops or question marks.

B Draw several pictures, with speech bubbles, to complete this conversation between Jeev and Jake.

Are you coming to swimming club tonight, Jake?

What time does it start?

Fairy Stories unit **2**

Writing

Key words

We use information books to find out facts. If you write notes from information books, you should not copy out every word. You should write the most important words. These are called **key words**. This is the first paragraph of 'The Grimm Brothers', with the key words underlined:

Many <u>fairy tales</u> are familiar to us thanks to two <u>German brothers</u>, called <u>Jacob</u> and <u>Wilhelm Grimm</u>. <u>Jacob</u> was <u>born</u> in <u>1785</u> and <u>died</u> in <u>1863</u>. <u>Wilhelm</u> was <u>born</u> in <u>1786</u> and <u>died</u> in <u>1859</u>.

A 1 Look at the other three paragraphs of 'The Grimm Brothers' on page 10. Write the key words from each paragraph.

2 Draw a table like the one below. Fill it in, using all the key words from 'The Grimm Brothers'.

Facts about Jacob	Facts about Wilhelm	Facts about the stories

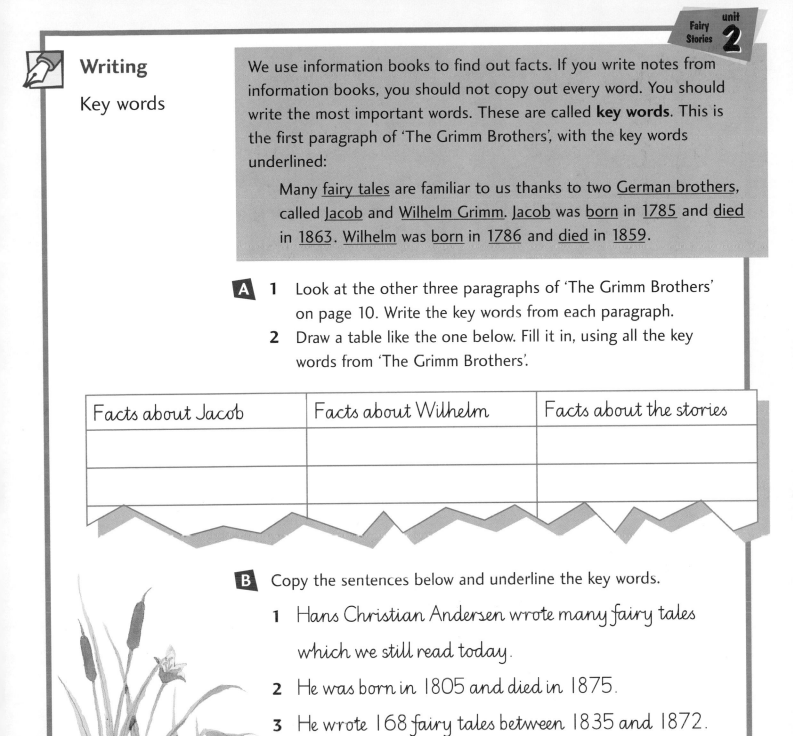

B Copy the sentences below and underline the key words.

1 Hans Christian Andersen wrote many fairy tales which we still read today.

2 He was born in 1805 and died in 1875.

3 He wrote 168 fairy tales between 1835 and 1872.

4 Some of his best known fairy tales are 'The Ugly Duckling' and 'The Tinder Box'.

Rabbits

Wild rabbits

Wild rabbits often live in large groups. They live in networks of burrows and tunnels under the ground, called rabbit warrens.

This diagram shows a rabbit warren.
a *The main entrance, which is open at all times.*
b and **c** *Smaller entrances, leading to nests, can be closed when the mother is away.*
d *A young female rabbit making a new nest.*
e *Rabbits do their droppings away from the warren so as to keep it clean.* ▼

In a warren there are usually lots of young rabbits to be kept warm and safe. Each doe (female rabbit) can give birth to up to seven litters a year, with four or five young in each litter. It is important, therefore, that the warren is built to keep the young away from danger.

Pet rabbits

Many people enjoy keeping rabbits as pets. There is a variety of different breeds, including lopeared, Netherland dwarf, chinchilla, large white and Belgian.

Pet rabbits are usually kept in wooden hutches. Rabbit hutches are sometimes too small for the size of rabbit being kept. They can also be dirty and damp. This is not kind. Pet rabbits, just like wild rabbits, like to keep themselves clean. It is important for them to have clean, fresh and dry bedding every few days, and the chance to exercise in a bigger run, as well as being given a good supply of food and fresh water.

◀ *This rabbit is enjoying some exercise, watched carefully by his owner.*

Comprehension

A Write a sentence to answer each question.

1 What is the name of a wild rabbit's home?
2 What is a female rabbit called?
3 In the diagram, there is a main entrance. How many smaller entrances are there?
4 What are pet rabbits usually kept in?
5 Write the names of two breeds of pet rabbit.

B 1 Find three words that describe what is often wrong with rabbit hutches.
2 Find three words that describe the kind of bedding tame rabbits need.
3 Find three words that show what the rabbit enjoys doing in the run.

C Using the information from the diagram, write some sentences about a rabbit warren.

Vocabulary

Alphabetical order

Remember, to put words into **alphabetical order**, you need to look at the first letters.

A Write each group of words in alphabetical order.

1 warren   rabbit   young

2 safe   warm   dry

3 food   water   bedding

To put into alphabetical order words that all begin with the same letter, you need to look at the second letter of each word. For example:

a<u>b</u>out   a<u>c</u>orn   a<u>d</u>der   a<u>e</u>roplane   a<u>f</u>ter

B Sort these groups of words into alphabetical order.

1 object   odd   occur   oats

2 dry   dirty   damp   dug

3 warren   whistle   wild   wean

Spelling

'le' words

Remember, to add 'ing' to a word that ends with 'e', remove the 'e' before adding 'ing'.

The 'le' letter pattern is often found at the end of a word. For example:
A coup<u>le</u> of litt<u>le</u> rabbits were in troub<u>le</u>.

A Copy each group of words below, then underline the word in each group that has a different spelling pattern from the others.

1 grumble   tumble   apple   stumble

2 bramble   scramble   ramble   little

3 thistle   tingle   bristle   gristle

B Copy each sentence, adding 'ing' to the 'le' word in green.

1 The baby rabbit liked <u>nestle</u> against its mother.

2 The rabbits were <u>scramble</u> back into the burrow.

3 Their food supply was <u>dwindle</u>.

Grammar

Verbs

Remember, a **verb** is an 'action' word. In a sentence, a verb tells us what is being done. For example:
> The rabbits <u>sleep</u> in their burrows.

A Write down all the words from the box that are verbs.

> jump   rabbit   hop   skip   warren
>
> dig   run   young   nibble   scratch   seven
>
> tumble   damp   grumble

B Copy these sentences. Underline the verbs.

1 Wild rabbits live in large groups.

2 They often eat farmers' crops.

3 A rabbit digs with its strong front legs.

4 The doe rabbits feed their young.

5 The boy strokes his pet rabbit.

Speech marks are sometimes called inverted commas.

Remember, when we write the exact words someone has spoken, we use **speech marks** (" ") around the words that were said. For example:

"My favourite type of rabbit is the Netherland dwarf," said Matthew.

A Write down the words that were actually spoken in each of these sentences.

1 "Can I build a hutch?" Matthew asked his dad.

2 "Yes, but make sure it is big and strong," Dad replied.

3 "I will," said Matthew.

4 "Can you help me, Dad?" he asked.

5 "Not now, but when I get home tomorrow evening," answered Dad.

B Look at the speech bubbles in the pictures below. Write down what is being said and who says it. Remember to use speech marks for the actual words a person said. The first part has been done to help you.

1 "Be careful with that hammer," warned Dad.

Writing

Simple reports

Look at the passage 'Rabbits' on pages 16-17. The writer has read about rabbits in information books and has used the information to write this **report**.

- The report has two parts. The first part is about wild rabbits. The second part is about pet rabbits.
- The writer has used a diagram with labels to show what a rabbit warren looks like.
- The writer has used a picture with a caption. The caption tells the reader more about the picture.

A Look at the labelled diagram of the rabbit warren on page 16. Using the information in the second part of the report, draw a labelled diagram of a good rabbit hutch.

B Choose one of the following types of animal to write about:

- dog
- cat
- hamster

Write a report about the type of animal you have chosen. You may already know something about this type of animal, but you may need to look in information books as well.

Write four paragraphs, one about each of the following:

1 where the animal lives/sleeps;

2 what the animal eats;

3 how the animal should be looked after;

4 the names of different breeds of the animal.

A Contents Page

This is the contents page of an information book about the weather.

Contents

Comprehension

Write your answers to these questions about the weather book.

A
1. In which section of the book could you read about thunder and lightning?
2. On what page does section 3 begin?
3. What could you read about in section 2?
4. How many pages are there in section 5?
5. On what page does section 8 begin?

B
1. What do you think the Introduction will tell you about?
2. What do you think the Further Reading section tells you about?
3. What does 'weather forecasting' mean?
4. Why do you think the book has a glossary?

C
1. In which section would you be most interested? Why?
2. In which section would you be least interested? Why?

Vocabulary

A thesaurus

Remember, **synonyms** are words that mean the same, or nearly the same.

If you can't think of the right word to use in your writing, a **thesaurus** might help you. A **thesaurus** is a book giving the **synonyms** of common words. The words are in alphabetical order. For each word, there is a list of synonyms and the **antonym**, if it has one. The antonym of a word means the opposite.

Below are some thesaurus entries.

| antonym | synonyms |

cold (hot) cool, chilly, frosty, icy, wintry, arctic

colour hue, tint, shade, tone, tinge, complexion

come (go) arrive, appear, reach, approach, enter, advance

comfortable (uncomfortable) warm, cosy, snug, contented, relaxed

contain hold, carry, enclose, include

correct (incorrect) right, exact, true, proper, accurate

A Use the thesaurus entries above to answer these questions.

1   Which word beginning with 'ch' means 'cold'?
2   Which word beginning with 's' means 'comfortable'?
3   Which word beginning with 'h' means 'contain'?
4   What is the antonym of 'hot'?
5   What is the antonym of 'come'?
6   What is the antonym of 'comfortable'?

Remember, the **antonym** word means the opposite.

B Copy these sentences, replacing the blue words with more suitable ones that mean the same thing. Use the thesaurus entries above to help you.

1   There is a cold wind today.
2   The sky can be different colours of blue.
3   The forecast says that the storm will come here soon.
4   Weather forecasts aren't always correct.
5   It is not comfortable when the weather is very hot.

Spelling

'ea' letter pattern

The 'ea' letter pattern makes two different sounds. For example:

I like to be on the b<u>ea</u>ch in the hot w<u>ea</u>ther.

A Choose a rhyming word from the box to match each word below. The first one has been done to help you.

bread	cream	peach	feather	pheasant	feast ✓

1 east   *feast*   2 weather   3 teach
4 head   5 team   6 pleasant

B Use each pair of words to write a funny sentence. The first one has been done to help you.

1 tea   flea   A fat <u>flea</u> jumped in Mum's <u>tea</u>.

2 steam   stream   3 wealthy   healthy

4 leather   feather   5 teach   reach

6 leap   heap   7 bead   lead

Grammar

Verb families

try	fall
tried	dries
blow	dried
fell	blowing
trying	blew
dry	falling
tries	drying
falls	blows

Verbs can be put into **verb families**. The names of verb families start with 'to', for example:

to jump   to run   to sing

In the sentence 'The weather forecaster <u>looks</u> at the clouds.', 'looks' tells us what the forecaster is doing. The verb family name is 'to look'. Verbs in the 'to look' family are:

look   looks   looked   looking

A Draw a table like the one below. Write each verb from the box on the left under the correct family name in the table.

to dry	to fall	to blow	to try

Remember, 'tense' means 'time'.

B Copy these sentences, changing the tense of each verb so that each sentence is about an action that happened yesterday. The first one has been done to help you.

1 I sit in the sun.   I sat in the sun.

2 I sing in the rain.

3 I hold the umbrella for Gran.

4 I swim in the sea.

Punctuation

Ending sentences

An **exclamation** is when somebody says something surprising, shocking, angry or unexpected.

A **full stop** (.) goes at the end of most sentences.
A **question mark** (?) goes at the end of a sentence that is a question.
An **exclamation mark** (!) goes at the end of a sentence that is an exclamation. For example: coming!

A hurricane is coming.

What is coming?

Help, a hurricane is coming!

A Copy these sentences and add the correct punctuation mark at the end of each one.

1 Help, I'm stuck __

2 Can we get through the snowdrift __

3 Ouch, that hurt __

4 It was too cold to go out __

5 Was that lightning __

B Write six sentences of your own, two that finish with an exclamation mark, two that finish with a question mark and two that finish with a full stop.

Writing

Contents pages

The sections of a book are often called **chapters**.

At the beginning of a book you often find a **contents page**. This page tells you what you will find in the book and on which page each section starts.

Each section of a book tells you about something different.

The contents page on page 22 is from a book about the weather. Each section is about a different type of weather.

A Imagine you are writing the contents page for a book about sport. Make a list of five different sports. Each chapter will be about one of the five different sports. Write the contents page. Set it out like the contents page on page 22. Include an introduction, a glossary, a further reading list and an index. The introduction of the book should start on page 3. Think about the page number where each chapter will start. Imagine that each chapter is 10 pages long.

B Imagine you are writing the contents page for a book about just one type of sport. Think about:
- how many chapters to have and what to call them;
- which page each chapter will start on and how long it will be;
- the other sections of the book (e.g. introduction, glossary, index, etc.).

Set out the information like the contents page on page 22.

A Day at the Zoo

Yes, but in a zoo they are given lots of fresh food! Animals never starve in a zoo, like they do in the wild!

Oh do stop arguing you two! Let's get to the shops or you won't get any food for your tea!

Comprehension

A Copy the sentences below. Fill in the missing words.

1 Meera and Sanjeev had been to the _____.

2 They saw _____ _____ in a cage.

3 Meera thought the animals were _____ and _____ in their cage.

4 Sanjeev said that the animals couldn't _____ free, _____ trees or _____ _____ things to eat.

B Write a sentence to answer each question.

1 Think of one more reason why animals should be kept in zoos.

2 Think of one more reason why animals should not be kept in zoos.

3 Do you agree with Meera or with Sanjeev?

C Draw a table like the one below and fill it in. Use Meera's and Sanjeev's views and some of your own.

Why animals should be kept in zoos	Why animals should not be kept in zoos

Vocabulary

Using a dictionary

Remember, a **dictionary** is useful for checking the spelling of words. To make them easier to find, the words are in **alphabetical order**. To sort into alphabetical order words that begin with the same letter, you need to look at the second letter of each word. For example:

baboon   bear   bird   boar   buffalo

a b c d e f g h i j k l m n o p q r s t u v w x y z

A Sort each group of words into alphabetical order.

You will need to look at the second letter of each word.

1	cow	crocodile	camel	cheetah
2	dog	duck	dingo	deer
3	antelope	alligator	ape	aardvark

Dictionaries also tell us the **definitions** (meanings) of words.

B Use a dictionary to find the definition of each word.

1 argue   2 zoo   3 forage   4 starve

Spelling

Suffixes

Remember, a **suffix** is a word ending. Adding a suffix to a word can change the meaning. For example:

help   helping   helped   helpful   helpless   helper

Be careful! Sometimes you need to change the word slightly when adding a suffix.

A In the box are some suffixes. Use the suffixes to make as many new words as possible from each word below.

| less | ful | ed | ing | er | ly | ness |

1 hope   2 love   3 happy   4 use

B Use each pair of words below in a sentence of your own.

1 careful careless   2 calmly calmer

3 sadly sadness   4 kinder kindness

Grammar

Adjectives

Adjectives are describing words. They tell us more about nouns. They can tell us about things like size, shape and colour. Adjectives can add detail and make your writing more interesting. For example:

old gorilla

adjective	noun

cramped cage

adjective	noun

young cubs

adjective	noun

A Choose from the box the adjective that best describes each of the nouns below.

tiny fierce long tall brown clever

1 _____ flea   2 _____ bear   3 _____ snake

4 _____ monkey   5 _____ giraffe   6 _____ tiger

You can use more than one adjective to describe a noun. For example:

<u>huge</u> <u>black</u> gorilla

<u>wrinkled</u> <u>old</u> elephant

<u>noisy</u> <u>colourful</u> parrots

B Look at this picture. Write some pairs of adjectives to describe the nouns in the picture, for example:

<u>cuddly</u> <u>white</u> rabbits

31

Punctuation

Capital letters

Every sentence starts with a **capital letter**. Proper nouns also start with capital letters, and so does 'I' when it is used as a word. For example:

| Beginning of a sentence | 'I' as a word |

When we went to Bristol Zoo, I sat next to Chloe and Mrs Jones on the coach.

| Proper nouns |

A Write down:

1   a   your full name
    b   the name of a relative or friend
    c   the name of the town or village where you live
    d   the name of your teacher.
2   Write two sentences about your favourite animal.

B Copy these sentences and add the capital letters and full stops.

1   mrs jones asked me to look after chloe

2   the coach took over an hour to reach bristol

3   we were in mr raja's group with ben, sean, nisha and sarah

4   first he took us to see the african and indian elephants

5   most of all, chloe and i liked the tigers

Writing

For and against

What you think about something is your **opinion**. People can have different opinions:

Some people in your class might think that it is a good idea to wear school uniform. They are 'for' wearing uniform.

Some people in your class might think that it is a bad idea to wear school uniform. They are 'against' wearing school uniform.

You must have reasons for your opinion. Meera was 'for' animals being kept in zoos. She gave her reasons. Sanjeev was 'against' animals being kept in zoos. He gave his reasons.

A Think about fox hunting. Write two headings in your book:

For	Against

Now write all the reasons you can think of:
- for fox hunting
- against fox hunting.

B Choose one of these:
- wearing school uniform
- watching television
- eating sweets.

Write the headings 'For' and 'Against' and write as many reasons under each heading as you can.

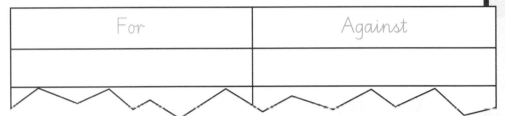

The Vanishing Key Trick

You will need:

a safety pin
a piece of elastic about 30 cm long
a key

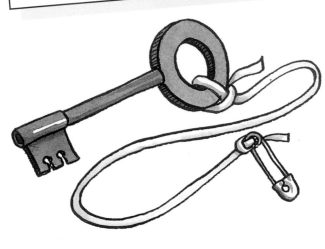

1 Tie one end of the elastic to the key and attach the other end to the safety pin.

2 Fasten the safety pin inside your right sleeve, near the shoulder, so that the key hangs down inside.

3 Adjust the length of the elastic so the key hangs out of sight, about 3 cm up your sleeve.

4 You need to practise making the key 'vanish'. Pull the key out of your sleeve a little. Hold it in your open right hand with your right thumb and first finger. Make sure the elastic is hidden behind your hand. Let go of the key so that it whizzes back up your sleeve.

5 To perform the trick, display the key, held between the thumb and first finger of your right hand. Make sure the elastic is behind your hand and out of sight. Close your right hand and cover it with your left hand. Let go of the key, which will whizz back up your sleeve without the audience seeing this happen. Show your empty left hand. Slowly open your empty right hand. The key has vanished!

Comprehension

A 1 What are these instructions for?
2 How many things do you need to do this trick?
3 What do you have to do with the elastic?
4 Where do you fasten the safety pin?
5 How do you practise making the key vanish?

B 1 Why do you think the instructions are numbered?
2 Would the trick work if you muddled up the numbered instructions?
3 Are the pictures useful? Why?
4 Do you think these instructions are easy or difficult to follow? Why?

C Draw three pictures to show what you have to do to perform the vanishing key trick (stage 5 of the instructions).

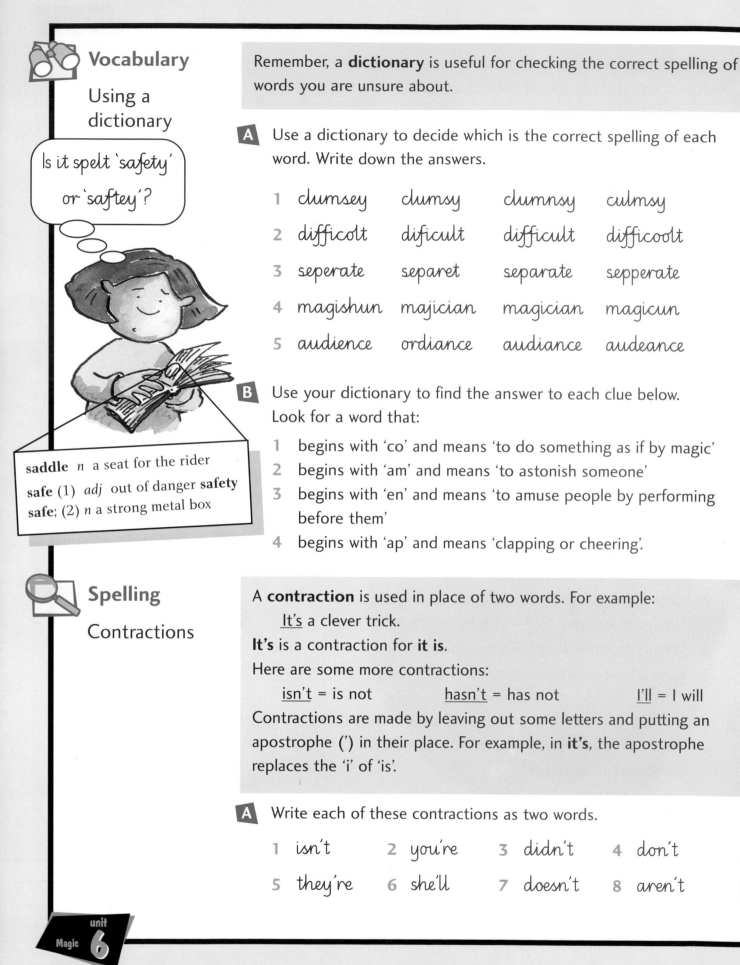

Vocabulary

Using a dictionary

Is it spelt 'safety' or 'saftey'?

saddle *n* a seat for the rider
safe (1) *adj* out of danger **safety**
safe; (2) *n* a strong metal box

Remember, a **dictionary** is useful for checking the correct spelling of words you are unsure about.

A Use a dictionary to decide which is the correct spelling of each word. Write down the answers.

1	clumsey	clumsy	clumnsy	culmsy
2	difficolt	dificult	difficult	difficoolt
3	seperate	separet	separate	sepperate
4	magishun	majician	magician	magicun
5	audience	ordiance	audiance	audeance

B Use your dictionary to find the answer to each clue below. Look for a word that:

1 begins with 'co' and means 'to do something as if by magic'
2 begins with 'am' and means 'to astonish someone'
3 begins with 'en' and means 'to amuse people by performing before them'
4 begins with 'ap' and means 'clapping or cheering'.

Spelling

Contractions

A **contraction** is used in place of two words. For example:
  It's a clever trick.
It's is a contraction for **it is**.
Here are some more contractions:
  isn't = is not   hasn't = has not   I'll = I will
Contractions are made by leaving out some letters and putting an apostrophe (') in their place. For example, in **it's**, the apostrophe replaces the 'i' of 'is'.

A Write each of these contractions as two words.

1 isn't	2 you're	3 didn't	4 don't
5 they're	6 she'll	7 doesn't	8 aren't

B Copy each sentence, replacing the purple words with a contraction.

1 I will show you a really clever trick.

2 I know you will never guess how it is done.

3 I have done it lots of times so I am good at it now.

Grammar

Adjectives

Remember, **adjectives** tell us more about nouns. They can tell us about colour. For example:

The magician had a <u>red</u> cloak.

A Look at this picture of a magician. Match each colour adjective in the box to one of the nouns below. Write down the answers.

red	white	green	yellow	purple	blue

1 _____ cloak   2 _____ rabbit

3 _____ curtains   4 _____ hair

5 _____ and _____ box

Sometimes we use other adjectives with colour adjectives to give more detail. For example:

The **bright** <u>red</u> lights shone on the **dark** <u>blue</u> box.

B Use each word from the box with a colour adjective in a sentence of your own. For example:

Karen is wearing a <u>bright pink</u> jumper.

deep	light	bright ✓	gentle	rich	dark

Remember, we use **capital letters** to start sentences and for proper nouns. For example:

> The trick baffled Ronan and Maria.

We also use capital letters in the titles of books, plays, films, etc. We use a capital letter for the first, last and all important words in the title. Words such as a, an, and, but, by, for, in, of, on, from, the, to, are not 'important' words in titles, so do not have a capital letter. For example:

> 'Instructions for the Vanishing Key Trick'

Remember, **proper nouns** are names of people, places or special days.

A Copy these book titles, adding capital letters where they are needed.

1 the bumper book of magic

2 the magic ring

3 alice in wonderland

4 how to fool your friends

5 mr marvel's book of tricks

You need capital letters to start sentences, for proper nouns and for titles.

B Copy these sentences, adding all the missing capital letters.

1 annie was given a book called learn to be a conjuror in one day.

2 my favourite magic book is called my ten greatest tricks, which was written by rudy walker.

3 have you ever read danny the champion of the world by roald dahl?

4 when I was younger i liked a book called bedtime stories for frances by russell hoban.

5 spike milligan's poem called the land of the bumbley boo really makes me laugh.

Writing

Instructions

Instructions are very important. Instructions tell us how to do things like cooking, caring for pets, playing games, etc.

Instructions have to be easy to understand. They are often written in short, simple sentences. Instructions are usually divided into numbered stages. This shows the order we need to do things.

A Look at these pictures. They show you how to make a jam sandwich. The sentences that go with the pictures are muddled up. Match each sentence with the correct picture and write them in the correct order.

1

2

3

Cut the sandwich in half.

Spread jam on one slice of bread.

Spread butter or margarine on each slice.

Cut the pieces in half again.

Get two slices of bread.

Press the two slices of bread together.

4   5   6

B Write instructions for doing one of the following things:
- cleaning your teeth
- getting a meal for your pet
- washing your hair.

The Maze Game

The object of the game:

You have to get from the start of the maze to the centre of the maze. If you come to a dead end, you have to go back the way you came. The first player to reach the centre of the maze is the winner.

In the box you will find:
the game board
red cards
1 dice
6 playing pieces
1 direction spinner

CENTRE

START

How to play:

1   Each player chooses a playing piece and puts it at the square marked 'Start' on the gameboard.

2   Each player rolls the dice in turn. The player who rolls the highest number goes first. Take turns to move the number of squares you scored on the dice.

3   When you get to a junction, spin the direction spinner to see which way to turn. If the spinner tells you to go in a direction that you cannot take, spin it again.

4   If you come to a dead end, you must miss a turn and go back the other way at your next turn.

5   If you land on a red square, you must pick up a red card and follow the instructions.

6   When you are six or fewer squares from the centre of the maze, you must roll the exact number needed to reach the centre.

Comprehension

A   Write a sentence to answer each question.

1   Where does your playing piece go at the start of the game?
2   Who goes first?
3   What should you do when you get to a junction?
4   What happens if you land on a red square?
5   What happens if you come to a dead end?

B   1   How many people can play the game at one time?
2   What does 'the object of the game' mean?
3   In your own words, explain how you can win the game.

C   The red cards give you instructions to follow. One of the cards says 'You cannot move again until you throw a 6.' Write three more red cards for the Maze Game.

Vocabulary

Definitions

Words that sound the same and are spelt the same are called **homonyms**.

Some words are spelt the same but have more than one meaning. Below is an entry in a dictionary. If a word has two or more different **definitions**, they are numbered.

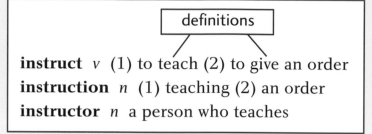

instruct *v* (1) to teach (2) to give an order
instruction *n* (1) teaching (2) an order
instructor *n* a person who teaches

This entry shows that 'instruct' and 'instruction' both have two definitions.

A Imagine that you are writing a dictionary. Write your own definition for each word.

1 dice   2 game   3 square
4 door   5 winner   6 maze

B 1 Here are some more words from the passage on pages 40–41. They all have more than one meaning. Write at least two definitions for each word.

a instruction   b box   c object
d play   e back   f miss

2 Copy the definition from a dictionary for each of these words. Next to each definition, write a synonym of the word.

a edge   b centre   c spin

d reach   e exact   f win

Remember, **synonyms** are words with the same, or a very similar, meanings.

Spelling

Singular and plural nouns

When we talk about only one thing, it is **singular**. When we talk about two or more things, they are **plural**. Usually, we add 's' to make a noun plural. For example:

singular: **plural:**
game   + 's' =   game<u>s</u>

A Write the plural of each word.

1 board 2 piece 3 square 4 door

5 centre 6 winner 7 player 8 number

If a noun ends with 's', 'x', 'ch' or 'sh', we add 'es' to make it plural.
For example:

singular: **plural:**
box   + 'es'=   box<u>es</u>
bush   + 'es'=   bush<u>es</u>

B Write the plural of each word.

1 fox 2 wish 3 bus 4 torch

5 table 6 church 7 instruction 8 flash

Grammar

Singular and plural sentences

Words can be made **plural**, and so can whole sentences. To change sentences from singular to plural, we sometimes need to change some of the words. For example:

The <u>child</u> <u>is</u> playing the <u>game</u>.
The <u>children</u> <u>are</u> playing the <u>games</u>.

A Copy these sentences into your book, changing them from singular to plural. The first one has been done to help you.

1 The boy had a new game for Christmas.

The <u>boys</u> had <u>some</u> new <u>games</u> for Christmas.

2 His sister likes to play the game.

3 She wins most of the time.

B Change these sentences from plural to singular.

1 The men play football every Saturday.

2 Their children go to watch.

3 The men travel to the matches in cars.

Sentence construction

Essential words only

To make our writing more interesting we sometimes add words. For example:

> They played the game.
> They enjoyed playing Josie's new game.

Sometimes, especially when writing instructions, it is better to keep sentences short, with only the essential words. For example:

> Take turns to roll the dice.

A Write each of these sentences in a shorter way, using fewer words.

1 First, when you are ready to play, turn on your computer and read very carefully indeed the instructions that will come up on the screen.

2 Jenny really liked playing her brand new game very much indeed.

3 All of her friends thought that she was extremely lucky to be given a new computer game that must have cost her parents a lot of money.

B Write these long, clumsy sentences in a shorter way.

1 If you and several of your friends want to play the game, you will need to make very sure that all the people who will be playing know exactly what they can do and what they can't do, or there will be arguments.

2 It is always best when you are playing a game with several of your friends if you make sure that all the people are arranged around the computer so that they can all see very clearly and all the people can reach the mouse when it is their turn to have a go.

unit **7**
Mazes

44

Writing

Rules

When we play games, there are **rules** to tell us what is and is not allowed. For the game to work, and to be fair, all the players must follow the rules.

Like instructions, rules have to be easy to understand. They are often numbered and are written in short sentences. Sometimes, rules are a list of 'DOs' and 'DON'Ts' – things you can and can't do.

When we visit public places, there are often rules about what you can and cannot do. For example, if you visit a farm, there are rules you should follow.

DO
- close the gates after you
- be quiet near farm animals
- walk on footpaths when you cross fields
- keep away from farm machinery

DON'T
- leave litter
- climb fences or barbed wire
- throw anything into farm ponds
- light fires

A Think of one reason for having each of these rules. Write the rule and the reason for it in one sentence. The first one has been done to help you.

DO

- *I should always close gates after me to stop farm animals getting out.*

A Write down a list of DOs and DON'Ts for one of the following:

- crossing the road
- cooking in the kitchen
- looking after a guinea pig.

Dirty Hands

This flow diagram shows how germs can pass from our hands into our bodies.

1

There are germs everywhere.
Every time you touch something,
you get germs on your hands.

2

You cannot see the germs, but
they are there!

3

If you touch food without washing your hands
first, the germs go on to the food.

4

When you eat the food, the germs go into your mouth.

5

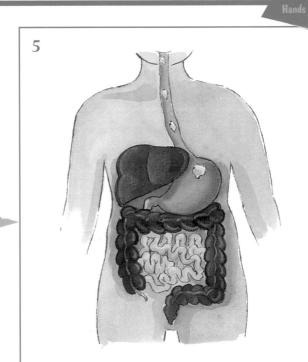

When you swallow the food, you swallow the germs as well.

Comprehension

A
1   Look at picture 1. What are the hands doing?
2   Look at picture 2. What do the hands have on them now?
3   Look at picture 3. What are the hands doing?
4   Look at picture 4. What is the boy eating as well as the sandwich?
5   Look at picture 5. What two things have gone into the boy's stomach?

B Write a sentence to answer each question.
1   What should the boy have done between pictures 2 and 3? Why?
2   Why do you think it is bad for us to swallow germs?

C Draw the flow diagram showing a big germ visible in all the pictures!
In picture 1, the germ will be on the football. Where will you draw the germ in the other pictures?

Vocabulary

Antonyms

Remember, **antonyms** are words that have opposite meanings.
For example:

dirty   clean

yes   no

A   Replace each coloured word with a word from the box that is its antonym.

1   after lunch

2   back door

3   finish eating

4   bottom drawer

5   blunt knife

6   soft cheese

7   correct answer

8   spend money

9   forget something

10   neat room

11   left hand

12   old clothes

> wrong   top   hard   sharp   save   right   new
> before   begin   remember   front   messy

B   We sometimes use pairs of antonyms when we are talking. Write a sentence using each pair of antonyms below. The first one has been done to help you.

1   in and out   Mum said she didn't want us running in and out all day.

2   high and low

3   up and down

4   come and go

5   on and off

Spelling

Compound words

Sometimes, two words are put together to make a new word, called a **compound word**. For example:

play + ground = <u>playground</u>

A Look at the flow diagram on pages 46-47 and find a compound word that begins with:

1 some   2 can   3 with

B Add another word to each word below to make a compound word.

1 time   2 every   3 snow

4 clock   5 bed   6 fire

7 water   8 foot   9 farm

Grammar

Singular and plural verbs

Notice that plural **verbs** <u>don't</u> have an 's' at the end.

If one person is doing something, the verb is **singular**. If two or more people are doing something, the verb is **plural**. For example:

Singular: The girl <u>strokes</u> the kitten.
Plural: The girls <u>stroke</u> the kitten.

A Copy these sentences, choosing a singular or plural verb to fill each gap.

1 The boy <u>wash/washes</u> his hands.

2 The boys <u>wash/washes</u> their hands.

3 Meena <u>eat/eats</u> with dirty hands.

4 Ali, Rupert and Will <u>eat/eats</u> with dirty hands.

5 Ali <u>feel/feels</u> sick.

6 Meena, Will and Rupert <u>feel/feels</u> sick too.

B Write a sentence of your own using each of these verbs.

1 clean   2 cleans   3 sit   4 sits

Sentence construction

Using 'is', 'was', 'are' and 'were'

We use 'is' and 'was' in sentences about **one** person or thing.
We use 'are' and 'were' in sentences about **more than one** person or thing. We also use 'are' and 'were' when we use 'you'. For example:

Janie <u>is</u> ready.
<u>Are</u> you ready?
All the children <u>are</u> ready now.

A Copy these sentences. Choose the correct word to fill each gap.

1 Chris <u>was/were</u> sick last week.

2 He <u>is/are</u> not often ill.

3 He and his brothers <u>was/were</u> all ill.

4 Their father <u>was/were</u> off work too.

5 You <u>is/are</u> not to go to their house yet.

6 They <u>is/are</u> all feeling better now.

B Write down the word from the box that belongs in each gap.

is	was	are	were

The children ___1___ finishing off their work. Joe ___2___
ready for his lunch.

Joe said, "I wish we ___3___ playing football today."

"We ___4___!" said Ben.

"You ___5___ going to be late," said their teacher.

"I ___6___ ready five minutes ago," said Ben.

"Well, what ___7___ all this mess on the table, then?"
asked his teacher, crossly.

Writing

Flow diagrams

Diagrams help us to explain things clearly. **Flow diagrams** show things happening one after another, in the correct order. A flow diagram has arrows, so you know which way to read it. The flow diagram 'Dirty Hands' on page 46–47 shows one way that germs get into our bodies. You can use flow diagrams for many different things.

Below is some information about how a tadpole turns into a frog. The stages are jumbled up.

A Write out the information in the correct order.

B Draw a flow diagram with labels, to show a tadpole turning into a frog.

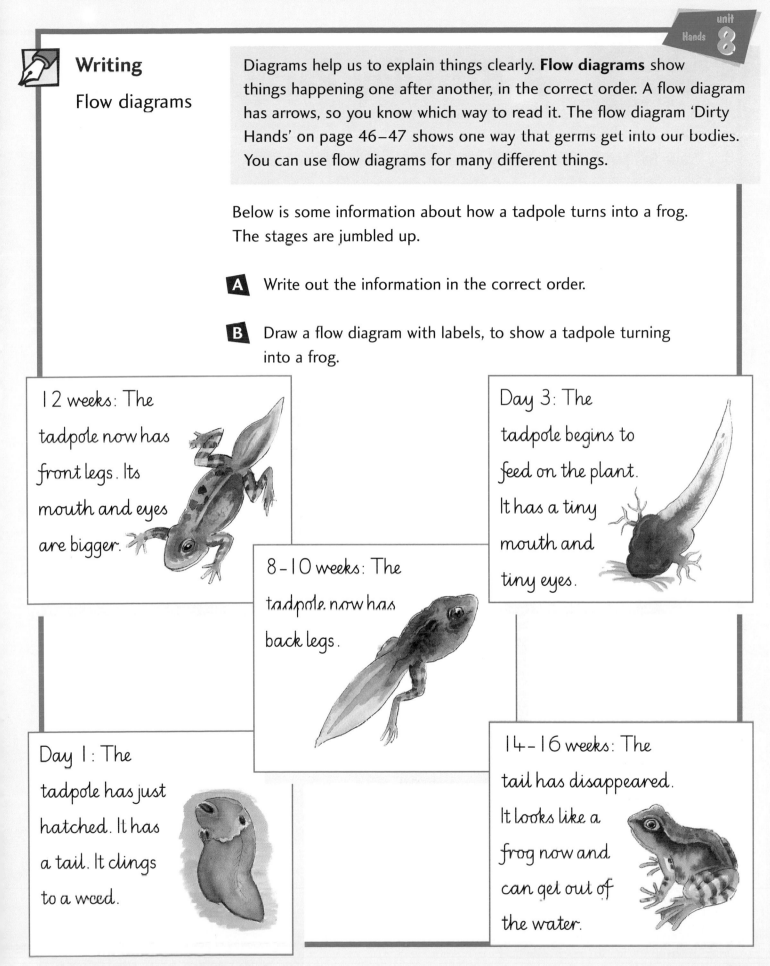

12 weeks: The tadpole now has front legs. Its mouth and eyes are bigger.

Day 3: The tadpole begins to feed on the plant. It has a tiny mouth and tiny eyes.

8–10 weeks: The tadpole now has back legs.

Day 1: The tadpole has just hatched. It has a tail. It clings to a weed.

14–16 weeks: The tail has disappeared. It looks like a frog now and can get out of the water.

A Birthday Party

Claire has just had her eighth birthday. She received lots of cards and presents, and had a wonderful birthday party. This is a letter she wrote to her Aunty Sue, to thank her for her present and tell her about the party.

77, Long Lane
Mapping
Yorkshire
MU5 5QX

17th September

Dear Aunty Sue,

Thank you for the lovely skirt you sent me for my birthday. It fits really well and I wore it at my party.

I invited some of my friends from school and they all came and they brought me some fantastic presents. We played lots of games. Dad made up a treasure hunt for us. After that, we danced to really loud music.

There was loads to eat and drink. My birthday cake, which was in the shape of a dinosaur, was great. All my friends had some. I have saved a piece for you to have when you come at the weekend.

Lots of love,

Claire

Comprehension

A
1 Who is the letter written to?
2 Who is writing the letter?
3 Where does the writer live?
4 How many paragraphs are there in the letter?

B Look at each paragraph of the letter. Copy and complete the table.

Paragraph	What it is about
1	the skirt
2	
3	

C Imagine you are Claire. Write two more paragraphs for the letter. What do you think Aunty Sue might like to read about?

Vocabulary

Common expressions

'Thank you' is an **expression** we use when someone has been kind or helpful. For example:

Thank you for the lovely skirt you sent me.

A Below are some expressions people often use. Use each one in a sentence of your own. The first one has been done to help you.

1 I'm sorry   I'm sorry I broke the cup.

2 be careful   3 be quiet

4 I'm fed up   5 watch out

B Think of two expressions you might use in a letter if you wanted to:

1 thank someone for something
2 tell someone you were feeling cross
3 apologise that you haven't done something that you should have done.

Spelling

Words within words

Spelling is often easier if you can find smaller words within a longer word. For example:

dearest   dear   ear   a   are   rest

A 1 Write all the smaller words you can find in each of the following words.

   a hearing   b fearsome   c nearby

2 Which two small words can you find in all of the words in question 1?

B Find a word that includes the 'ear' letter pattern to match each of these definitions. The first one has been done to help you.

1 a smudge   smear
2 at the back   3 someone loved
4 to be afraid   5 twelve months

Grammar

Pronouns

Remember, a **pronoun** is a word that can be used instead of a noun. **Personal pronouns** are used in place of nouns that stand for people.
For example:

> her   we   I   you   him   she   they   he
> <u>Claire</u> saved a piece of cake for <u>Aunty Sue</u>.
> <u>I</u> have saved a piece of cake for <u>you</u>.

> pronoun for 'Claire'   pronoun for 'Aunty Sue'

A Copy these sentences. Choose a personal pronoun from the box to use in place of the pink words in each sentence.

> they
> he
> her

1 My mum said my new skirt would suit my mum.

2 All of my friends said that my friends liked it.

3 My dad said that my dad liked the colours.

Some pronouns are called **possessive pronouns**. They tell us who has or owns something. For example:

> his   hers   mine   ours   theirs   yours
> This skirt is <u>Claire's</u>.
> This skirt is <u>hers</u>.   possessive pronoun for 'Claire'

B 1 Write a possessive pronoun that could be used in place of the pink words in each sentence.

a The baby thought the present was for him, but it was for me.

b I haven't got a CD player. Can we use your CD player?

c Claire told her brother that the party was her party.

2 Write a sentence using each pair of possessive pronouns.

a yours   mine   b his   hers   c hers   ours

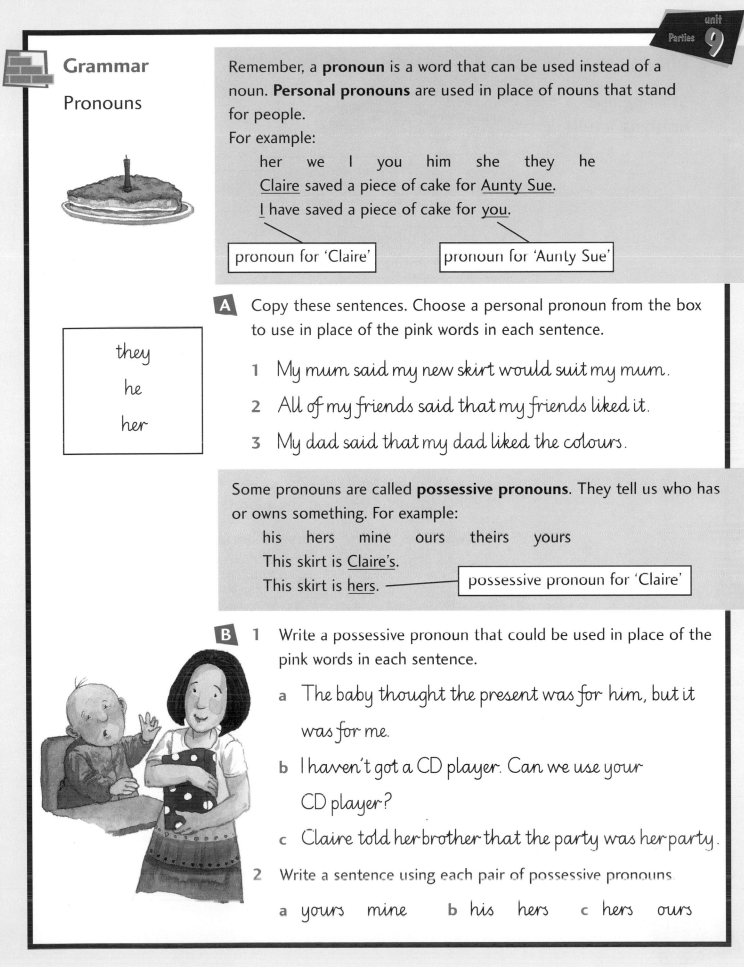

🔗 Punctuation

Starting and finishing letters

At the top of a letter to a friend or relation, you write:

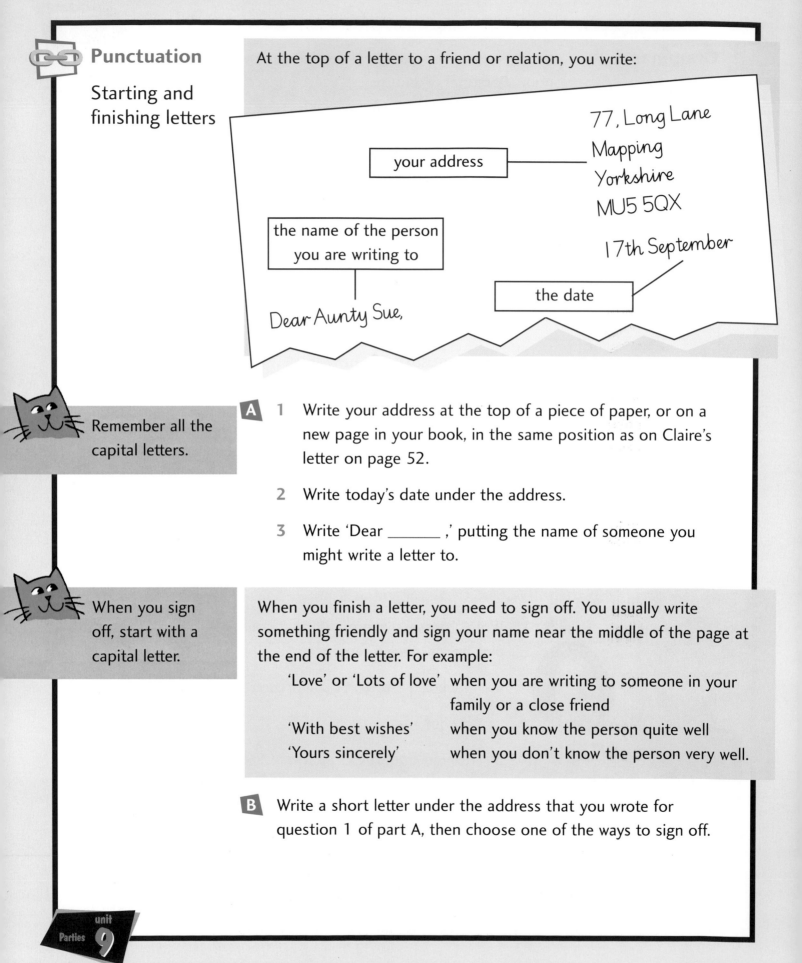

your address → 77, Long Lane
Mapping
Yorkshire
MU5 5QX

17th September

the name of the person you are writing to

the date

Dear Aunty Sue,

Remember all the capital letters.

A 1 Write your address at the top of a piece of paper, or on a new page in your book, in the same position as on Claire's letter on page 52.

2 Write today's date under the address.

3 Write 'Dear _____ ,' putting the name of someone you might write a letter to.

When you sign off, start with a capital letter.

When you finish a letter, you need to sign off. You usually write something friendly and sign your name near the middle of the page at the end of the letter. For example:

'Love' or 'Lots of love' when you are writing to someone in your family or a close friend

'With best wishes' when you know the person quite well

'Yours sincerely' when you don't know the person very well.

B Write a short letter under the address that you wrote for question 1 of part A, then choose one of the ways to sign off.

Writing

Letters

We write **letters** for lots of different reasons, for example, to:

- ask something;
- complain about something;
- explain or tell somebody something;
- congratulate someone.

Balbir is going to visit her grandparents in India. She has written the letter below, to say she is looking forward to seeing them.

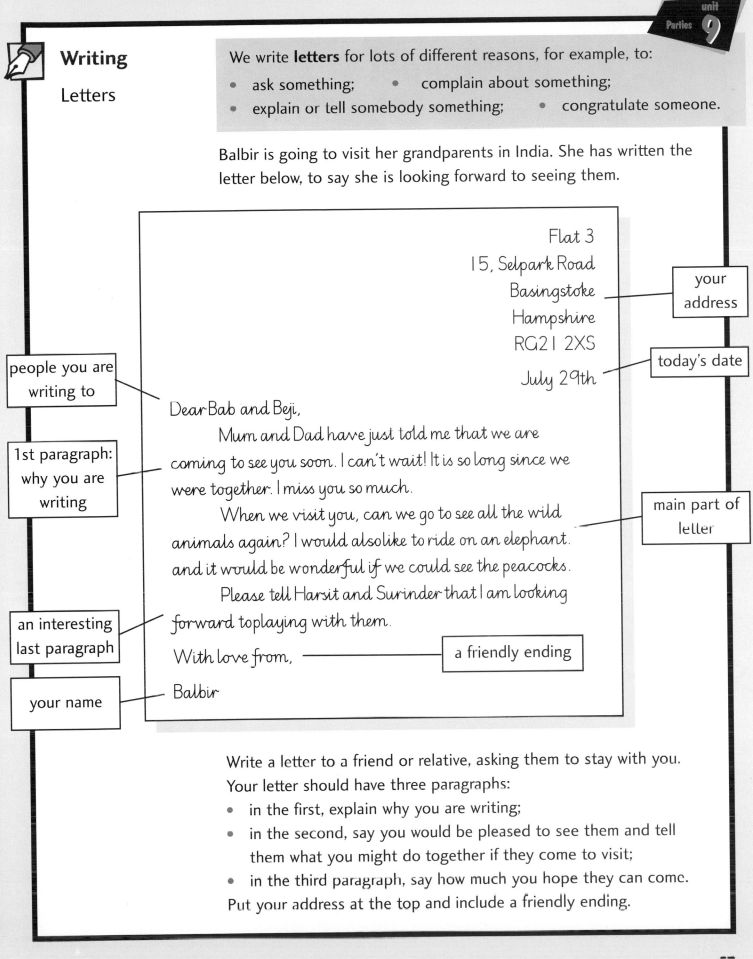

Flat 3
15, Selpark Road
Basingstoke
Hampshire
RG21 2XS

July 29th

Dear Bab and Beji,

Mum and Dad have just told me that we are coming to see you soon. I can't wait! It is so long since we were together. I miss you so much.

When we visit you, can we go to see all the wild animals again? I would also like to ride on an elephant. and it would be wonderful if we could see the peacocks.

Please tell Harsit and Surinder that I am looking forward to playing with them.

With love from,

Balbir

Labels:
- your address
- today's date
- people you are writing to
- 1st paragraph: why you are writing
- main part of letter
- an interesting last paragraph
- a friendly ending
- your name

Write a letter to a friend or relative, asking them to stay with you. Your letter should have three paragraphs:

- in the first, explain why you are writing;
- in the second, say you would be pleased to see them and tell them what you might do together if they come to visit;
- in the third paragraph, say how much you hope they can come.

Put your address at the top and include a friendly ending.

31st October

MITCH CAUSES CHAOS

from Jo Taggart, our special reporter

Hurricane Mitch left a trail of disaster as it ripped through towns and villages in Nicaragua yesterday. The violent winds and torrential rains brought terrible floods and huge mudslides, burying villages and leaving many people homeless. Thousands are missing, many are feared dead.

With so much damage, the rescue services hardly knew where to begin. In most towns, the main buildings, including hospitals, have gone – swept away! It is going to take years, and a great deal of help from the rest of the world, if the country is ever to recover from this terrible disaster.

Comprehension

A 1 Who wrote the report?

2 What is the name of the hurricane?

3 Which adjective describes:
   a the winds?
   b the rains?
   c the floods?
   d the mudslides?

4 Why are the rescue services finding it so difficult?

5 As well as the rescue services, who else is going to have to help?

GLOSSARY

torrential in a rushing stream
mudslides mixtures of rainwater and mud

4th November

My dearest Grandpa,
I don't know how to tell you this.
Our lovely house, our garden, our
car – they have all gone. They were
washed away in the most terrible
flood that has ever hit our village.
The wind was so strong when we
went to bed that we were scared.
Dad said it would soon stop, but it
didn't! I think he didn't want us to
worry, but he was the most worried
of us all, I could tell.
    Then, in the night, there was a
great roaring noise, so we all ran out
of the house and up the hill just

(1)

This letter was written by a young
survivor of Hurricane Mitch.

before a huge wave of mud and
water hit the village. We were
shivering and frightened. I've never
been so frightened. Now we have
nothing – everything has been
washed away.
    Mum says we are lucky – at least
none of our family has been hurt.
Some people were badly hurt, and
some have even been killed.
    We are living in a tent at the
moment, so we have no proper
address. I'll write again soon.
All my love,
Miguella

(2)

Comprehension

B 1 Who is the letter written to?
2 Who has written the letter?
3 Which adjective describes:
   a the house? b the flood? c the wind? d the wave of mud?
4 How was the writer feeling when she had to run 'out of the house and up the hill'?
5 Why is there no address at the top of the letter?

C The newspaper report and the letter are both about Hurricane Mitch. Write whether it
is the report or the letter that:
1 tells you how the hurricane affected lots of people;
2 tells you how the hurricane affected one family;
3 tells you what the rescue services are trying to do for everybody;
4 tells you what happened to Miguella's family;
5 does not tell you how the writer is feeling;
6 tells you how the writer is feeling.

Adjectives

Remember, **adjectives** are describing words. They can also be used to compare things. For example:

    A cyclone is a <u>strong</u> wind.

    It is <u>stronger</u> than a gale.

    It is the <u>strongest</u> of all winds.

Adjectives that compare two things usually end with 'er'. Adjectives that compare three or more things end with 'est'. If the adjective ends in 'y', we change the 'y' to 'i' before adding 'er' or 'est'.

For example:

    hap<u>py</u>   happi<u>er</u>   happi<u>est</u>

Adjectives that compare two things are called **comparative adjectives**. Adjectives that compare three or more things are called **superlative adjectives**.

Be careful! Some words end with 'y'.

A   Copy and complete this table of comparing words.

	+ 'er'	+ 'est'
wet	wetter	
fast		fastest
	rainier	
windy		windiest

If the adjective is a long word, and doesn't end in 'y', we usually write 'more' in front of it if it is a comparative adjective and 'most' if it is a superlative adjective, instead of adding 'er' or 'est'.

For example:

    Cyclones can cause <u>terrible</u> damage.

    The latest cyclone caused <u>more terrible</u> damage than the one last year.

    Cyclones can cause the <u>most terrible</u> damage of all winds.

B Copy these sentences, but change each adjective into a comparative adjective by adding 'more' or 'most'. The first one has been done to help you.

1 This is a <u>powerful</u> cyclone than the last one.

This is a <u>more powerful</u> cyclone than the last one.

2 It is the <u>frightening</u> cyclone we have had for many years.

3 Predicting cyclones is a <u>important</u> job than predicting sunny weather.

4 Hurricane Mitch was the <u>terrible</u> storm for many years.

5 It caused the <u>devastating</u> damage of any storm in the past hundred years.

Spelling

Prefixes

Remember, a **prefix** is a group of letters put on the front of a word to change its meaning. For example:

| happy | <u>un</u>happy |
| place | <u>mis</u>place |

A Copy these words and underline the prefixes.

1 anticyclone   2 impossible   3 cooperate

4 disappeared   5 misbehave   6 untie

7 invisible   8 nonsense   9 preview

B Use a dictionary to help you write three other words beginning with each of the prefixes you found in part A. The first one has been done to help you.

1 anti   anticlimax   anticlockwise   <u>anti</u>cipate

Grammar

First, second and third person

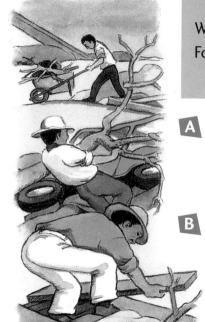

We use the **first person** when we are writing about ourselves.
For example:

> <u>I</u> don't know how to say this.

We use the **second person** when we are talking directly to the reader.
For example:

> <u>You</u> will not be able to imagine the damage.

We use the **third person** when we are writing about other people.
For example:

> <u>They</u> will take years to rebuild the city.

A Imagine that you were trapped by an unexpected flood. Write a few sentences for your diary, using the first person. For example, 'I felt really scared as …'

B 1 Use the second person to write brief instructions describing how to build a shelter if your home was destroyed in a hurricane. For example, 'To build a shelter, you need …'

2 Use the third person to write about some problems the people of Nicaragua will have to cope with after Hurricane Mitch. For example, 'The people of Nicaragua will not have …'

Punctuation

Ending sentences

Remember, we use a **full stop** (.) to end most sentences, but we use a **question mark** (?) at the end of a question, and an **exclamation mark** (!) at the end of an exclamation.

A Copy these sentences, adding the missing punctuation marks.

1 "Quick_ Get out of the house_" screamed Mum_

2 "Help_ Help_" shouted a voice close by_

3 I realised that my friend was trapped_

4 "What can we do_" I asked Mum and Dad_

B Look at part A. Write some sentences about what might have happened next. Make sure you use correct punctuation.

Writing

Points of view

We can write about something that happens from different **points of view**.

When Hurricane Mitch happened, reporters went to see the villages it had hit and wrote reports for their newspapers.

A newspaper report will give you the facts. News reporters write about **what happened to other people**. Hurricane Mitch affected lots of people.

People who lived in the villages wrote letters to let their friends and relatives know that they had survived. The people wrote those letters about **what happened to them** and to their families and close friends.

A You are a reporter and have to write a story about a volcano that has erupted. Hot ash and lava have covered a village at the bottom of the volcano. The people knew it was going to erupt, so they had left the village. No one was hurt, but all the houses were destroyed.

B Now imagine that you were one of the people from the village. Write a letter to a friend, describing what happened and how you felt.

Finding a Book

There are two main types of books: Fiction books contain stories or poems. Non-fiction books contain facts. Most libraries keep fiction and non-fiction books in separate areas.

Fiction and poetry

Fiction books are arranged on the shelves so that all the books by an author are put together. All the books by Roald Dahl should be next to each other, and all the books by Leila Berg will be together. There are many different authors so, to help you find the books more easily, the books are set out in alphabetical order, using the author's surname. Leila Berg's books will come before Roald Dahl's books because B comes before D in the alphabet.

Non-fiction

A library will have hundreds of non-fiction books. When you are looking for an information book, the author is less important than the subject of the book. It is useful if all the books on one subject are kept together. Librarians use a system of numbers to help you find the book you want. They write or print a number on each non-fiction book and arrange the books on the shelves in number order. Most libraries use the same numbers for the subjects. This system of numbers was worked out by Melvil Dewey over 100 years ago. Below are the numbers of some of the subjects you might need to find.

0 to 99	Encyclopedias and dictionaries
100 to 199	Ideas and thinking
200 to 299	Books about religion
300 to 399	Books about transport, customs, police
500 to 599	Books about birds, animals, science, mathematics and stars
600 to 699	Books about houses, homes, farming, electricity
700 to 799	Books about painting, drawing, music, sport
900 to 999	Books about countries and history

Your library probably has lots of books on mathematics and science, which all begin with a 5. Looking at the second digit of the number will help you to find the exact subject you want.

510 are books about maths

520 are about the sun, planets, moon and stars

530 are about magnets and electricity

540 are about chemistry

550 are about rocks

560 are about dinosaurs and fossils

570 are about the human body

580 are about trees and flowers

590 are about birds and animals

Comprehension

A Copy and complete these sentences.

1 Books that contain stories and poems are called _____ books.

2 Books that contain facts are called _____ books.

3 Fiction books are put on the shelves in _____ order.

4 Non-fiction books have _____ on them to help you find what you are looking for.

5 _____ _____ invented this system of numbers.

B Write the numbers of non-fiction books on the following subjects. The first one has been done to help you.

1 going to church   200 to 299

2 dairy cows   3 buses and trains

4 tigers   5 playing the recorder

C Look at the numbers for maths and science books – 510 to 590. Which number would be written on each of these books?

1 *Looking at Rocks*   2 *Wild Flowers of Britain*

3 *The Planet Mars*   4 *Number Machines*

5 *How Your Body Works*   6 *Big Book of Fossils*

Vocabulary

Using a dictionary

The word 'book' is a **homonym** – it has more than one meaning.

This is the entry in a dictionary for the word 'book':

book (1) *n* a number of sheets of paper bound together in a cover; (2) *v* to reserve, as to book seats in a cinema

definitions

an example of the word being used

n = noun   *v* = verb

A Write these words in the correct alphabetical order.

| shuttle | slack | saturate | shift | seal | science |

B Look up each of the words from part A in two or three dictionaries. Decide which definition you think is best, then write out each word with its definition, as if you were writing your own dictionary.

Spelling

'ary', 'ery', 'ory' word endings

Words that end with 'ary', 'ery' or 'ory' can be confusing to spell because they sound similar. For example:

libr<u>ary</u>	diction<u>ary</u>
slipp<u>ery</u>	nurs<u>ery</u>
hist<u>ory</u>	fact<u>ory</u>

A Use a dictionary to find out whether each of these words ends with 'ary', 'ery' or 'ory'. Write down the correct spellings.

1 machin___   2 necess___   3 st___

4 observat___   5 deliv___   6 prim___

7 discov___   8 mem___   9 Janu___

Remember, to make the **plural** of a word ending with a consonant, followed by a 'y', change the 'y' to 'i' before adding 'es'.

B Write the plural of each word.

1 library   2 dictionary   3 mystery

4 memory   5 burglary   6 discovery

7 story   8 secretary   9 nursery

Grammar

Using 'am' and 'are'

'Am' is used when you write about **one person**. For example:

I <u>am</u> finding a book.

'Are' is used when you write about **more than one person**.
For example:

They <u>are</u> finding their books.

'Are' is also used with '**you**', whether you are writing about one person or more than one person. For example:

You <u>are</u> looking on the wrong shelf.

A Copy and correct these sentences.

1 Is you coming to the library tonight?

2 We is in a hurry.

3 I are not sure if I can.

4 Mum and Dad is going out so I must look after
   my sister.

B Write down the missing words.

1 I _____ going to change my books.

2 Megan and Sophie _____ changing theirs, too.

3 I think I _____ going to get a book about butterflies.

4 They _____ looking for story books.

5 We _____ all pleased with the books that we
   have chosen.

Sentence construction

Conjunctions

Using **conjunctions** to join together short sentences is one of the easiest ways to improve your writing. For example:

> I spent a long time choosing a book. There are thousands of books in our library.

> I spent a long time choosing a book <u>because</u> there are thousands of books in our library.

Here are some useful conjunctions:

and	but	so	because	although	though	after	for
	until	yet	as	or	when	while	so

A Write down the conjunction used in each sentence.

1 The books are sorted on the shelves so all the books by an author are put together.

2 All the books by Roald Dahl should be next to each other, and all the books by Leila Berg will be together.

3 Leila Berg's books will come before Roald Dahl's because B comes before D in the alphabet.

B Write each pair of sentences as a single sentence. Use a different conjunction to join each pair of sentences.

1 Non-fiction books are sorted by subject. The subjects are more important than the authors.

2 I don't read many books. I do like reading a good story when I go on holiday.

3 The bookshelves are full. The librarian keeps buying new books.

4 Will you choose a book about volcanoes? Would you prefer a book about dinosaurs?

Writing

Using a library

After you have looked at a book, be sure to put it back in the right place or the next person won't be able to find it!

When you visit a **library** you are like a detective. You are looking for a book and you have to follow the clues!

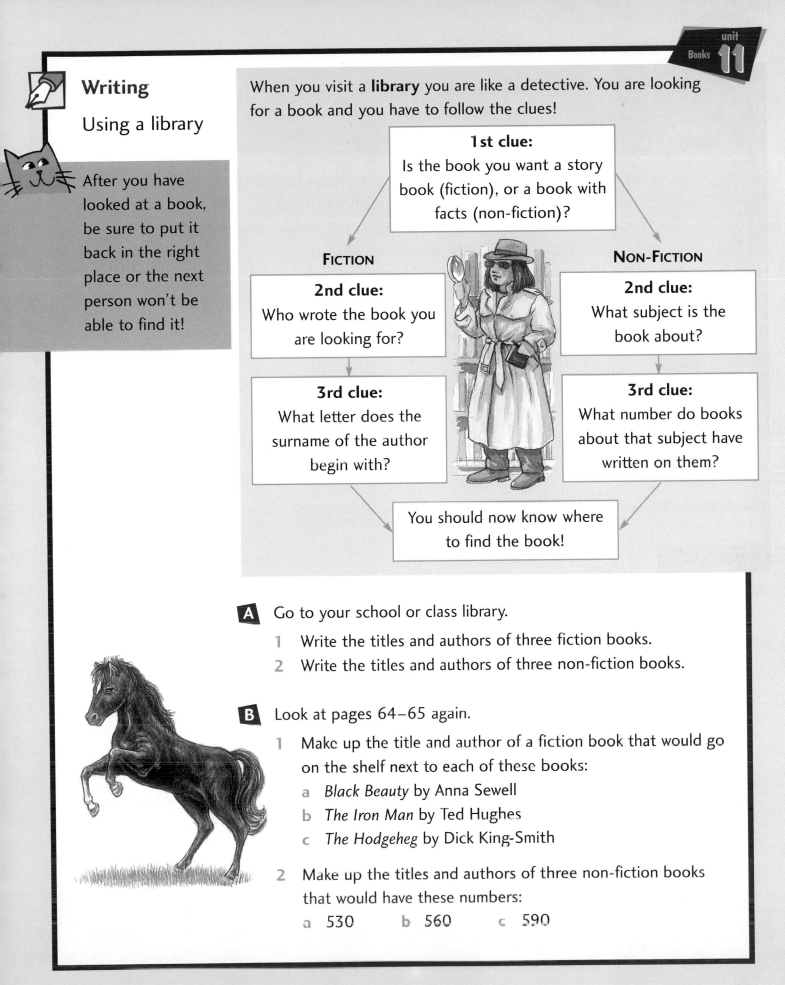

1st clue:
Is the book you want a story book (fiction), or a book with facts (non-fiction)?

FICTION

2nd clue:
Who wrote the book you are looking for?

3rd clue:
What letter does the surname of the author begin with?

NON-FICTION

2nd clue:
What subject is the book about?

3rd clue:
What number do books about that subject have written on them?

You should now know where to find the book!

A Go to your school or class library.

1 Write the titles and authors of three fiction books.

2 Write the titles and authors of three non-fiction books.

B Look at pages 64–65 again.

1 Make up the title and author of a fiction book that would go on the shelf next to each of these books:

a *Black Beauty* by Anna Sewell

b *The Iron Man* by Ted Hughes

c *The Hodgeheg* by Dick King-Smith

2 Make up the titles and authors of three non-fiction books that would have these numbers:

a 530   b 560   c 590

This is the index in a book called *All About Tea*. An **index** is a list of the main subjects covered in an information (non-fiction) book. It is at the end of the book. The main entries in an index are in alphabetical order. Sometimes, there are sub-sections of words under some of the main entries.

main words

INDEX

sub-section of main entry 'blends'

page numbers in the book where the information can be found

Comprehension

A Look at the index and answer these questions.

1 Which page will tell you about tea markets?
2 Which page will tell you about tea in Japan?
3 What will you find out about by reading page 12?
4 What will you find out about by reading page 21?
5 How many countries grow tea?

B 1 Why do you think information books need an index?
2 How is an index different from a contents page?

C Copy and complete this table, showing what is on pages 4, 5, 6, 7 and 8 of the book called *All About Tea*.

Page	What I will read about
4	
5	
6	
7	
8	

Vocabulary

Using an index

Use a dictionary to find out the meaning of any words that you are unsure about.

A In the box are entries for an index in a book about birds. Write the words in alphabetical order, as if they were in an index.

> eggs   feeding   flying   wings   nesting
> preening   tail   incubation   camouflage   bill
> plumage   feathers   chicks   migration
> mobbing   body   display

B Imagine that you are going to write a book about something that interests you, such as your hobby, a sport you like or your pet. Make a list of all the main subjects you would write about in your book. Write the list in alphabetical order.

Spelling

Letter blends

Letter blends are groups of letters that are often found together. For example:

fl:	flag	flap	flame	fleet	
str:	strip	strap	strand	strong	straight
st:	step	stop	steep	nest	must rusty

A Write four words that start with each of these letter blends.

   1 gr   **2** dr   **3** sl   **4** tr

B **1** Write four words that have these letter blends at the end or in the middle.

   a nd   **b** mp   **c** sk   **d** nt

   2 Write the word that goes with each clue below.

     a Starts with 'cr', comes in a packet and are crunchy to eat.
     b Starts with 'gr', and is a big smile.
     c Starts with 'sl', and is what you do in bed.
     d Starts with 'fl', and is the name for a group of sheep.
     e Starts with 'st', and is something a wasp might do to you.

Grammar

Nouns, adjectives and verbs

Remember:

A **noun** is the name of a person, place or thing.

An **adjective** tells us more about a noun.

A **verb** is an action word that tells us what is being done.

For example:

| verb | noun | | verb | noun |

William gulps fizzy lemonade while Mum sips hot tea.

| noun | adjective | | noun | adjective |

A **1** Think of an adjective to go with each of these faces.

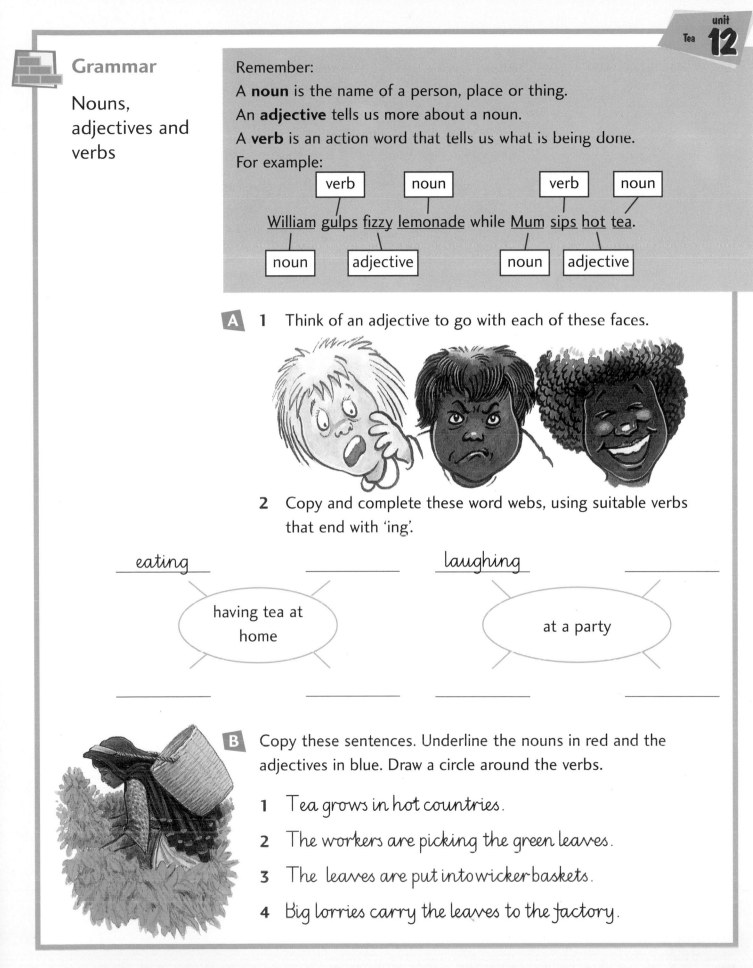

2 Copy and complete these word webs, using suitable verbs that end with 'ing'.

eating _____ laughing _____

(having tea at home)   (at a party)

_____ _____   _____ _____

B Copy these sentences. Underline the nouns in red and the adjectives in blue. Draw a circle around the verbs.

1 Tea grows in hot countries.

2 The workers are picking the green leaves.

3 The leaves are put into wicker baskets.

4 Big lorries carry the leaves to the factory.

Punctuation

Commas

A **comma** (,) is used to separate each word in a list. Instead of a comma, 'and' goes between the last two items in a list. For example:
There are several blends of tea including Assam, English Breakfast, Darjeeling, Earl Grey, Keemun and Russian.

A 1 Copy these sentences, adding the missing commas.

    a The countries where tea is grown include China Georgia Indonesia Japan and India

    b The book on tea has sections about planting growing picking drying and packing

    c The three main types of tea are black tea green tea and oolong tea

2 Write a sentence containing a list of your four favourite drinks. Remember to use commas correctly.

Commas also help the reader to understand the meaning of a sentence. They show where to make a short pause. For example:
Hasan's Gran, who loves her cup of tea, was upset when she ran out of milk.

B Write these sentences. Add commas to show where the reader should make a short pause.

1 Although he had run as fast as he could Hasan found that the shop was closed by the time he got there.

2 Gran who by now was getting thirsty was cross that the milk had run out.

3 Hasan knowing how much Gran wanted her tea said he would borrow some milk from a neighbour.

4 Gran was pleased with Hasan very pleased indeed.

Writing

Indexes

Remember, an **index** is an alphabetical list of the main subjects covered in a non-fiction book. An index helps you to quickly find the information you are looking for.

A 1 Here are some words to do with life in Tudor times. Write them out in alphabetical order, as if they were part of an index.

> Henry VIII   beggars   armour   food
> houses   wars   clothes   education

2 Find the names of the planets that go around our Sun. Don't forget the Earth! Write them in the order that you would find them in an index.

B The weather book in Unit 4 (page 22) was about:

> sun   wind   clouds   rain   hail   snow   thunder
> lightning   fog   mist   dew   frost   drought
> forecasting the weather

1 Arrange the subjects in alphabetical order, as you would find them in an index.

2 Look back at pages 22–27 and write the correct page number next to each entry in the list you wrote for question 1.

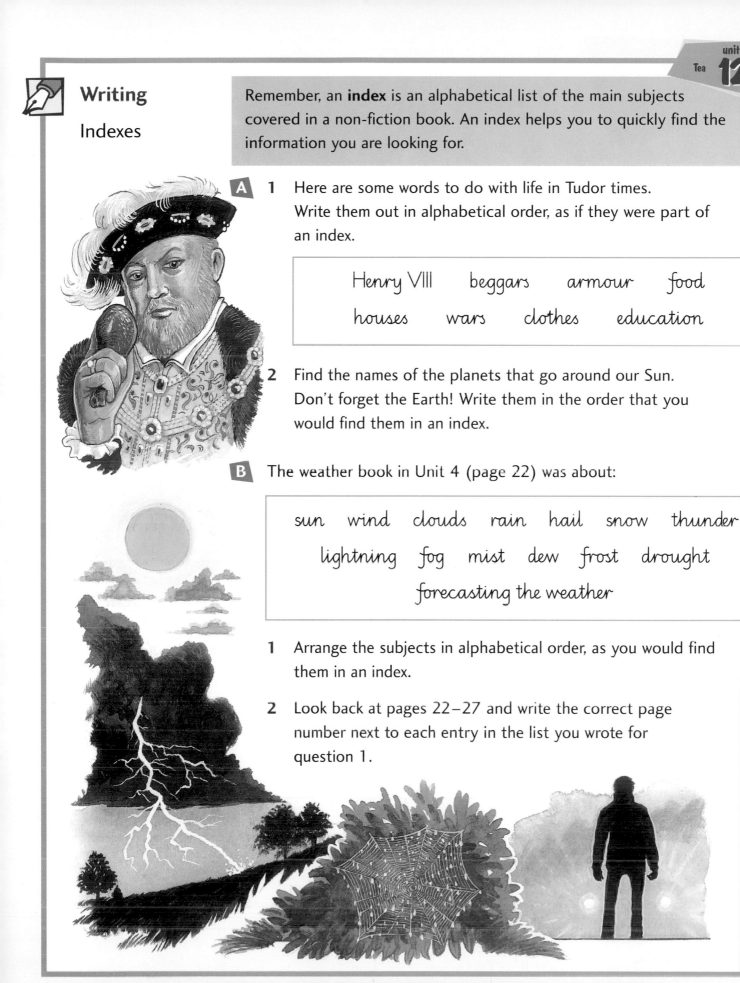

Check-up

Vocabulary

A Sort these letters and words into **alphabetical order**.

1 n g e p l s z q

2 house   roof   floor   window   garden

3 purple   blue   green   gold   pink

B Choose a **synonym** and an **antonym** from the box for each word below.

1 small   2 pretty   3 happy   4 correct   5 cold

chilly   attractive   little   cheerful   right
unhappy   incorrect   huge   hot   ugly

C Write these words in **alphabetical order**.

silly   heavy   hill   separate   fall   flow

D In your own words, write what each of these words means.

1 heavy   2 farm   3 maze   4 library   5 supermarket

E Copy and complete this table of **comparing words**.

	+ 'er'	+ 'est'
small		
	wider	
		heaviest
strong		
sleepy		
busy		

Spelling

A Use each of these **homophones** in a sentence of your own.

1 sail   2 sale   3 fort   4 fought   5 right   6 write

B Write two more words that have the same **spelling pattern** as each word below.

1 thread   2 beam   3 vole   4 toad   5 rail   6 hair

C Choose from the box three **suffixes** that can be added to each word below. Write the words with the **suffixes** added, being careful to spell them correctly.

less   ful   ed   ing   er   ly   ness

1 clever   2 tidy   3 correct   4 care   5 soft

D Write a **contraction** for each pair of words.

1 were not   2 had not   3 you will   4 it is   5 I have

E Write the **plural** of each of these words.

1 stream   2 brush   3 arch   4 fox   5 pass

F Add another word to each word below to make a **compound noun**.

1 every   2 bed   3 home   4 mill   5 times

G At least three little words are hidden in each of these words. Write them out.

1 everyone   2 because   3 farming   4 nearest   5 somebody

H Use a dictionary to help you to find three words that begin with each of these **prefixes**.

1 im   2 un   3 mis   4 non   5 anti

I Decide whether to add 'ary', 'ery' or 'ory' to complete each of these words.

1 hist___   2 necess___   3 nurs___   4 burgl___   5 fact___

Grammar

A Write down the words from the box that are **nouns**.

> train   fill   bus   fast   blue   car   ship
> floating   aeroplane   landed

B Copy each sentence, adding a **verb** to fill each gap.

1 The rabbits _____ into their burrow.

2 A strong wind _____ the washing on the line.

3 The magician _____ a clever trick.

4 Claire _____ me to her party.

5 I _____ the book I needed at the library.

C Choose the correct **verb** to complete each sentence.

1 The cows was/were grazing.

2 The train is/are late.

3 Some girls was/were playing netball.

4 These children is/are doing a project.

D Choose the best **adjective** from the box to describe each animal.

> fierce   cuddly   colourful   tall   huge

1 elephant   2 giraffe   3 kitten   4 wolf   5 parrot

E Copy this sentence and replace each group of coloured words with a **pronoun**.

Mr Brown asked Jasmin and Sue if they would carry the heavy case up the stairs for him.

Punctuation and sentence construction

A Copy these sentences, adding the missing capital letters and punctuation marks.

1 she climbed the ladder

2 jim fitted the roof tiles

3 have we brought the nails

4 quick, get help

B Copy these sentences, adding the missing speech marks.

1 Hold the rabbit tightly, said Richard.

2 Can I have a turn next? asked Sarah.

3 Wash your hands now, said Dad.

4 Please come when I call you! said Mum crossly.

5 We're coming, called the children.

C Copy these sentences, adding the missing capital letters.

1 our coach broke down in telford.

2 mrs briggs said i could help her.

3 roz, azfal, yasmin and sean caught the train to london.

4 i bought a book for aunty heather's birthday present.

D Write down the correct word to fill each gap.
Choose from the words in the box.

am	is	are

1 The children _____ fishing in the lake. Rob _____ first to catch a fish.

2 Polly says it _____ too small and should be put back.

3 Rob says, "Don't worry, I _____ going to."

4 "You _____ in a good place. I _____ coming to join you," said Pete.

5 The children _____ lucky and all of them catch a fish.

E Write your home address as it would be written at the top of a letter

Writing

A 1 Write the name of a sport or hobby that you enjoy or would like to try.

2 Imagine you are going to write a book about this hobby.

Design a book cover for your book. Remember to include:
- the title
- the author's name
- an illustration.

3 a Write a list of things to do with the hobby. Use the list to write a contents page for your book.

b Use the contents page you wrote to help you write a simple index for your book.

B 1 Make a list of reasons why you should go to bed early.

2 Make a list of reasons why you should not go to bed early.

3 Write a letter to your friend complaining about having to go to bed early.

Explain to your friend:

a the reasons why you are sent to bed so early

b the reasons why you think you should not go to bed at this time.

C Write instructions for doing one of the following:
- making a bed
- making toast
- playing your favourite playground game.